NO HANDS ALLOWED

A Robbie Reader

Abby Wambach

J B WAMBACH, A. ORR
Orr, Tamra
Abby Wambach

$17.95
CENTRAL   31994013978041

Tamra Orr

Mitchell Lane
PUBLISHERS

P.O. Box 196
Hockessin, Delaware 19707
Visit us on the web: www.mitchelllane.com
Comments? email us: mitchelllane@mitchelllane.com

Printing   1   2   3   4   5   6   7   8   9

A Robbie Reader
No Hands Allowed

Abby Wambach	Brandi Chastain	Brian McBride
DaMarcus Beasley	David Beckham	Freddy Adu
Jay-Jay Okocha	Josh Wolff	Landon Donovan
Michael Owen	Ronaldinho	Ronaldo

Library of Congress Cataloging-in-Publication Data
Orr, Tamra.
  Abby Wambach / by Tamra Orr.
    p. cm. — (A Robbie reader. No hands allowed)
  Includes bibliographical references and index.
  ISBN-13: 978-1-58415-601-7 (lib. bdg.)
  1. Wambach, Abby, 1980– —Juvenile literature. 2. Women soccer players—United States—Biography—Juvenile literature. 3. Soccer players—United States—Biography—Juvenile literature. I. Title.
  GV942.7.W36O77 2008
  796.334092—dc22
                                                                2007023468

ABOUT THE AUTHOR: Tamra Orr is a full-time writer and author living in the Pacific Northwest. She has written more than 50 books for children and families, including *Orlando Bloom, Ice Cube,* and *Jamie Foxx* for Mitchell Lane Publishers. She is a regular contributor to more than 50 national magazines and a dozen standardized testing companies. Orr is a mother to four and life partner to Joseph.

PHOTO CREDITS: Cover—AP Photo/Jacques Brinon; pp. 1, 3—Wang Jiaowen/Color China Photos/ZUMA Press; p. 4—Hong Shan/Imaginechina/ZUMA Press; p. 6—Ronald Martinez/Getty Images; p. 8—Stephen Dunn/Getty Images; p. 12—Tom Hauck/Getty Images; p. 14—Don Emmert/AFP/Getty Images; p. 16—Doug Pensinger/Getty Images; p. 18—Tim Sloan/AFP/Getty Images; p. 19—Vaughn Youtz/ZUMA Press; p. 20—Shaun Botterill/Getty Images; p. 22—Bryan Bedder/Getty Images; p. 24—Guang Niu/Getty Images; p. 25—Christof Koepsel/Bongarts/Getty Images; p. 26—Elsa/Getty Images.

ACKNOWLEDGMENTS: The following story has been thoroughly researched and to the best of our knowledge represents a true story. While every possible effort has been made to ensure accuracy, the publisher will not assume liability for damages caused by inaccuracies in the data. This story has not been authorized or endorsed by Abby Wambach.

TABLE OF CONTENTS

Just before she was injured, Abby Wambach competed for the ball with North Korea's Om Jong Ran in the 2007 FIFA Women's World Cup. The game ended in a draw, with a score of 2-2.

Unstoppable

Blood was dripping down her face and shoulders, but all Abby Wambach could think about was getting back out on the field.

It was the opening game for the Women's World Cup in September 2007. Wambach was determined to win against North Korea, even though she was already running with a sore right toe. Despite the discomfort, she took a pass from captain Kristine Lilly on the right side of the penalty area and shot the ball straight into the net. It was close! The **goalkeeper**'s gloves touched the ball but could not stop it.

Just a few minutes later, Wambach was defending a cross. She ran right into North Korea's Ri Kum-Suk. Wambach dropped to the ground, blood spurting from a deep cut on the

Bloody but determined, Wambach headed in for stitches.

back of her head. It was clear that she needed a doctor. As she left the field, North Korea scored a goal.

"When they scored right away as I went off, I started to get worried," said Wambach. "So I started to run to the locker room to get stitches put in."

Coach Greg Ryan had to decide whether to replace Wambach or wait for her to come back out on the field. "It was a very tough call," said Ryan. "The doctor said they could get her back within just a few minutes. Abby is such an important player to this team. I thought we could withstand playing 11 against 10."

"I really had to hurry up the process," said Wambach. "I was yelling at the doctors to get it done quicker. I . . . hurried up and got my jersey on and ran as fast as I could." With eleven stitches, she dashed back in the game, which ended in a 2-2 tie.

When the World Cup was over days later, Wambach's team had won the third-place bronze medal. She had scored a goal that earned the respect of her team and fans alike. First Lilly passed from the left sideline. Wambach played it against her chest and then hammered a left-footed shot from 12 yards inside the upper left corner on the near post. Former U.S. team captain Julie Foudy stated, "You just can't hit it any sweeter than that. It shows why she is one of the greatest players in the world right now. That's unstoppable; unbelievable the way she hit that."

Perhaps that is the perfect way to describe Abby Wambach on the soccer field—she is unstoppable. She has been right from the beginning.

Wambach is ready to play in the USA Women's National
Team's friendly match against Finland in August 2007.

No Fear

Splash! One by one, Beth, Laura, Peter, Matthew, Patrick, and Andrew Wambach dived into their swimming pool. Suddenly, two-year-old Mary Abigail, or "Abby," surprised everyone by climbing up on the diving board too.

"Even at that age, she had no fear," said Judy, Abby's mother. "I think the fact that she was the seventh of seven children had a lot to do with that. She wanted to **emulate** (EM-yoo-layt) everything her older sisters and brothers did. It didn't matter to her that Beth and Laura were 11 and 10 years older than she was."

It would be three more years before the Wambachs realized that their daughter was a true athlete. She joined a youth soccer league in their hometown of Rochester, New York.

Soon it was clear that she was the best player on the field. "Until then, we really didn't have any way to **gauge** how good she was because we had just seen her compete . . . against her older sisters and brothers," explained Pete, Abby's father. "But when you put her in a situation with her peer group for that first time, you couldn't help noticing the difference."

By nine, Abby was so advanced that she joined a boys' team for four years. "It was the only way she was going to truly develop her skills," said Judy.

Abby's love for sports went beyond soccer to basketball. When she was in her last years of high school at Our Lady of Mercy in Rochester, she was torn between the two sports, but in the end, soccer won.

"I'll never regret playing basketball," she says. "I think the leaping skills I developed going for rebounds has helped me become good at heading the ball in soccer. Plus, I don't believe it's healthy just concentrating on one sport year-round when you are young," she explained.

After high school, Abby went to the University of Florida. While she was there, she received many awards and was the school's all-time leading scorer. Soon, soccer became too demanding. "It stopped being fun for a while," she admitted. "It started feeling like a job. Luckily, I rediscovered my love for the game."

Even though Abby was still young, there was no doubt she was a great player. She had to decide whether to stay in college or become a **professional** (proh-FEH-shuh-nul) player. Her history of competing with her siblings helped her decide. "Looking back on it," she said, "being the youngest kid in a large family was a great proving ground for me. It forced me to become super competitive and made me more aggressive, and those traits have come in handy on the soccer field." Abby was ready to go full time!

The battle for the ball is on between Thori Bryan of the San Jose CyberRays and Wambach during the first half of their WUSA match at San Jose's Spartan Stadium in 2002.

The Most Valuable . . . Prankster?

In 2002, Abby was the second overall draft pick in the WUSA, or Women's United Soccer Association. She began playing for the Washington Freedom, and with her help, the team won the Founders Cup III. She was voted the game's Most Valuable Player.

While playing for the Washington Freedom, Abby got the chance she had been hoping for: playing with longtime idol Mia Hamm. Mia's outstanding playing helped the women's U.S. soccer team win gold in the 1996 Atlanta Olympics. By doing so, she inspired thousands of young girls—including Abby—to play the game.

Wambach and teammate Mia Hamm celebrate during a match between the China National and the U.S. Women's Soccer teams in 2004. Hamm retired later that year.

When Abby first joined the team, Mia was out with an injury. "When Mia returned," said her father, "the two of them clicked perfectly. Mia helped take the pressure off Abby and

Abby helped take the pressure off Mia. It's been quite a scoring combination."

The two players worked beautifully out on the field together. "Mia is the greatest friend anybody could ever have," said Abby. "I've learned a lot about soccer and about life being around her."

As much as Abby is known for her talent on the field, she is also loved for her sense of humor. "Before the games, I'm kind of a goofball," she admitted. "I'm always dancin', singing, anything to calm people down. I guess I'm really trying to keep myself calm too a little bit."

Kate Markgraf, another soccer player, stated, "She's Jekyll and Hyde. When we are out there, you won't find a more competitive player in the world. . . . If she doesn't come off the field with grass and bloodstains all over her uniform, she doesn't consider it a good game. In the locker room and on the road, she's always pulling pranks. We've gotten her back a few times, but she's the team leader in that category too."

15

During the 2003 WUSA match at Washington, D.C.'s RFK Stadium, Wambach and Nancy Augustyniak of the Atlanta Beat zero in on the ball. The game ended in a tie at 1-1.

To the World Cup

Abby's skills playing for the WUSA earned her a spot in the U.S. Women's National Team's training camp. Early in 2003, she found that her game was slipping a bit. Her coach, April Heinrichs, cut her from a match. She said that if Abby did not improve both her skills and her fitness, she would miss the World Cup.

"April and I have always had a good relationship," Abby recalled. "She knows I have pretty thick skin, coming from a big family. I could handle any sort of criticism. . . . I think a light bulb went off in my head." Abby improved right away–and made the World Cup.

No one could miss her on the field during the game against Norway. Teammate Cat Reddick fed her the ball, and Wambach scored

In a powerful aerial move, Wambach reaches for the ball during the 2003 Women's World Cup match against Sweden. In the World Cup match against Norway, she headed the ball into the goal.

the only goal on a header. The power forward called it the biggest goal of her life. She spent the rest of the game running over defenders and, as reporters phrased it, "generally wreaked havoc all over the . . . field."

Although the team did not win the Women's World Cup, they took home a bronze medal. "When you set your expectations on winning the whole thing and don't succeed, it's a huge blow," said Abby after the **tournament** (TOR-nuh-ment).

In September 2003, the WUSA had to close. Abby joined the U.S. Women's National Team for the upcoming 2004 Olympics in Greece. She was thrilled to be a part of it. "I remember watching the Olympics with my family when I was a young girl. I thought,

Wambach's love for the team and for winning is clear as she cheers a goal made by teammate Kristine Lilly during the 2003 FIFA Women's World Cup match against Canada. The winner of the match would bring home the bronze medal.

Wambach and teammate Julie Foudy celebrate Wambach's winning goal against Brazil during extra time of the Athens 2004 Summer Olympic Games in Greece. It was a gold medal win!

'Wow, I'd love to have the opportunity to experience that some day.'"

Training camp was hard work. Every day, the players had a two-hour field practice and a three-hour weight training session. "The mentality of the U.S. Women's National Team is that we're the fittest team in the world," said Abby. The average soccer player runs five miles every game! They must be able to sprint, stop, turn, and sprint again for 90 nonstop minutes. To do that takes a great deal of energy and practice.

At the Olympics, in minute 22 of extra time, Abby snatched a goal right into the roof of the net. When Kristine Lilly was given a free kick from the corner of the field, Wambach hit the ball with her forehead from 12 yards out. The win brought the U.S. a second Olympic title. Abby was **nominated** (NAH-mih-nay-ted) for the FIFA Women's World Player of the Year.

Later that year, she also got involved in **politics** (PAH-luh-tiks). She helped John Kerry run for U.S. president. Kerry lost the election, but Wambach gained another new experience.

21

Out of her usual grass-stained uniform, Wambach attends the 27th Annual Salute to Women in Sports awards dinner at New York City's Waldorf-Astoria Hotel in October 2006.

Making an Impact

Since 2005, Abby has been involved in playing **exhibition games** (ek-suh-BIH-shun GAYMS). She also works with the international organization Right to Play. This group uses sports as a way to help children in **disadvantaged** (dis-ad-VAN-tijd) areas of the world. Abby has gone to parts of Africa to meet some of these children. She works hard to raise money for the program as well. It has been a life-changing experience for her. "When I went to Africa, I gained so much personally and individually," she said. She hopes that in the future, she can continue to help children.

The lack of fear Abby has shown since climbing up on that diving board so many years ago still follows her. Coach Heinrichs once said

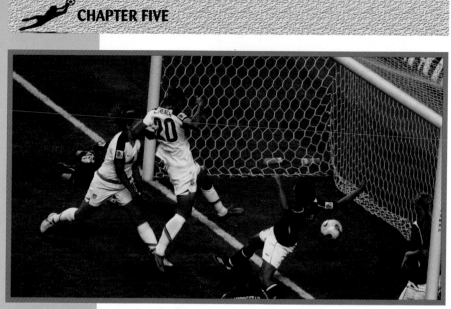

Wambach charges through to score a goal during the 2007 Women's World Cup between the U.S. and Norway in Shanghai, China.

of her, "Only the foreign players in the league know what's coming. Because chances are she's run over them like a Mack truck and left her license plate number on them."

Goalkeeper Briana Scurry said, "All I can say is that I'm glad Abby's on my team because seeing her coming at me with the ball and a head of steam is a scary sight."

Even Abby agrees. "Fearlessness is my best **attribute** [AA-trih-byoot]. I think. I'm not afraid to go into tackles or get dirty out

After the 2007 Women's World Cup, Brazil's Marta holds the Adidas golden shoe, Wambach the silver, and Norway's Ragnhild Gulbrandsen the bronze. These awards are given to the top goal scorers of the tournament.

there. . . . I like to go into battle and be in the middle of it."

Abby keeps her fans in mind at all times. She remembers a day long ago when her brother tried to get the autograph of a famous baseball player and was turned away. "That really made a big impression on me," she recalled. "I always said that if I were ever able to be a role model, then I would definitely take the

25

A photo before the international friendly match with Mexico in April 2007 shows the U.S. Women's National Team players (from back row, left to right): Stephanie Lopez, Abby Wambach, Lori Chalupny, Cat Whitehill, Hope Solo, Kristine Lilly, Carli Lloyd, Shannon Boxx, Lindsay Tarpley, Christie Rampone, and Heather Mitts.

extra time to make sure that all the kids were happy. It doesn't take that much time to say 'hello' or . . . to actually make a connection, whether it's eye contact or an actual conversation. . . . I set a goal for myself to try and make an impact with the fans."

On the field and off, Abby has achieved that goal. She definitely keeps making an impact.

26

1980 Mary Abigail Wambach is born on June 2 in Pittsford, New York.

1998 She graduates from Our Lady of Mercy High School in Rochester, New York. She is awarded the NSCAA Player of the Year and the Umbro Player of the Year.

1999 She plays for the University of Florida Gators and receives NSCAA first team All-American, NCAA National Champ, and freshman All-American awards, and is the university's all-time leading scorer.

2002 Abby is the second overall draft pick for WUSA. She begins playing for Washington Freedom; her team wins Founders Cup III; she is voted the game's Most Valuable Player.

2003 She goes to the World Cup, and her team brings home the bronze medal.

2004 Abby trains with the U.S. Women's National Team; they win a gold medal in the Summer Olympics in Athens. Abby campaigns for John Kerry for President.

2005 She plays in Algarve Cup in Portugal, and in exhibition games.

2006 She is nominated for the FIFA Women's World Player of the Year award.

2007 She helps her team win third place in the Women's World Cup.

attribute (AA-trih-byoot)—a trait or characteristic.

disadvantaged (dis-ad-VAN-tijd)—lacking the normal necessary things for life.

emulate (EM-yoo-layt)—to copy or imitate.

exhibition games (ek-suh-BIH-shun GAYM)—an unofficial game between professional teams that is played as part of training or as a fund-raiser.

gauge (GAYJ)—judge; measure.

goalkeeper (GOHL-kee-per)—player positioned in the goal box.

nominated (NAH-mih-nay-ted)—named as a choice to receive an award.

politics (PAH-lih-tiks)—the art or science of government.

professional (proh-FEH-shuh-nul)—someone who is paid to do a job.

tournament (TOR-nuh-ment)—a series of games that make up a single event, such as the Women's World Cup.

Books

Chastain, Brandi. *It's Not About the Bra: Play Hard, Play Fair and Put the Fun Back into Competitive Sports.* New York: HarperCollins, 2004.

The Stars of the WUSA. *WUSA Girl's Guide to Soccer Life.* Franklin, Tennessee: Cool Springs Press, 2003.

Zarzycki, Daryl. *Mia Hamm.* Hockessin, Delaware: Mitchell Lane Publishers, 2005; updated 2007.

Works Consulted

Associated Press. "Bloody Wambach Returns, Helps U.S. Gain Tie." MSNBC, September 11, 2007. http://www.msnbc.msn.com/id/20721786

DiVeronica, Jeff. "Amazing Abby Stuns Sweden in World Cup Play." *Rochester (N.Y.) Democrat and Chronicle,* September 15, 2007. http://www.democratandchronicle.com/apps/pbcs.dll/article?AID=/20070915/SPORTS/709150309/1007

ESPN Soccernet.com. "Wambach Propels U.S. Past Norway." October 1, 2003. http://soccernet.espn.go.com/wwc/report?id=120319

FIFA.com. "Abby Bleeds Red, White and Blue."
September 13, 2007.
http://www.fifa.com/womenworldcup/news/
newsid=595129.html

FIFA.com. "Wambach: Nothing Scares Me."
September 7, 2006.
http://www.fifa.com/en/print/article/
0,4039,121683,00.html

Goal.com. Interview: "Abby Wambach, U.S. Forward
& Right To Play Athlete Ambassador."
February 2, 2007.
http://www.goal.com/en-US/
articolo.aspx?contenutoid=224394

Hersh, Philip. "Wambach Bulls Her Way to Top;
Physical Forward an Unstoppable Force for U.S.
Team." *Chicago Tribune,* August 8, 2007.
http://www.topix.net/content/trb/2007/08/
wambach-bulls-her-way-to-top

McDowell, Dimity. "Scoring Machine: Soccer Player
Abby Wambach Is Going for the Gold." *Muscle
& Fitness/Hers,* May 2004.
http://findarticles.com/p/articles/mi_m0KGB/
is_4_5/ai_n6033416

Pitoniak, Scott. "Wambach Eager to Showcase Soccer Skills on Olympic Stage." *Rochester (N.Y.) Democrat and Chronicle*, August 7, 2004. http://www.usatoday.com/sports/olympics/ athens/soccer/2004-08-07-wambach_x.htm

Wade, Stephen. "U.S. Women Quickly Turn Attention from World Cup to Beijing Olympics." AP Sports, October 1, 2007. http://www.usatoday.com/sports/soccer/ 2007-10-01-2418683207_x.htm

Whiteside, Kelly. "Wambach Won't Back Down." *USA Today,* September 18, 2003. http://www.usatoday.com/sports/soccer/ national/2003-09-18-wambach_x.htm

Web sites

ESPN Soccernet
http://soccernet.espn.go.com

FIFA Women's World Cup
http://www.fifa.com/womenworldcup/

Official Web Site for Abby Wambach
http://www.abbywambach.com/

U.S. Olympic Team Player Biography
http://www.usoc.org/26_13777.htm

INDEX